ICE AGE MEGA BEASTS

MAMMOTHS

by Sara Gilbert

CREATIVE EDUCATION • CREATIVE PAPERBACKS

Published by Creative Education and Creative Paperbacks
P.O. Box 227, Mankato, Minnesota 56002
Creative Education and Creative Paperbacks are
imprints of **The Creative Company**
www.thecreativecompany.us

Design and production by **Chelsey Luther**
Art direction by **Rita Marshall**
Printed in the **United States of America**

Photographs by Alamy (Stocktrek Images, Inc.), Corbis (Mauricio Anton/
Science Photo Library, Mark Hallett/Stocktrek Images, Gianni Dagli Orti, Alice
Turner/Stocktrek Images), Dreamstime (Artesiawells, Tranac), FreeVectorMaps.
com, Getty Images (Dorling Kindersley, Jason Edwards, Mark Hallett Paleoart,
Print Collector), Shutterstock (Ozja)

Illustration on p. 21 © 2016 Michael Rothman

Library of Congress Cataloging-in-Publication Data
Gilbert, Sara.
Mammoths / Sara Gilbert.
p. cm. — (Ice age mega beasts)
Includes bibliographical references and index.
Summary: An elementary exploration of mammoths, focusing on fossil
evidence that helps explain how their big tusks and shaggy fur helped these
plant-eating beasts adapt to the last Ice Age.

ISBN 978-1-60818-767-6 (hardcover)
ISBN 978-1-62832-375-7 (pbk)
ISBN 978-1-56660-809-1 (eBook)
1. Mammoths—Juvenile literature. 2. Elephants, Fossil—Juvenile literature.
3. Prehistoric animals.

QE882.P8 G55 2017
569.67—dc23   2016014629

CCSS: RI.1.1, 2, 3, 4, 5, 6, 7, 10; RI.2.1, 2, 4, 5, 6, 7, 10; RI.3.1, 2, 4, 5, 7, 10;
RF.1.1, 2, 3, 4; RF.2.3, 4; RF.3.3, 4

First Edition HC 9 8 7 6 5 4 3 2 1
First Edition PBK 9 8 7 6 5 4 3 2 1

Contents

Furry Elephants

The sun is shining on the plains, but the ground is frozen. The woolly mammoth is hungry. It uses its strong trunk to grab onto grass.

Other mammoths lived when the woolly mammoth did, but they were not as widespread.

Mammoths were *ancestors* of elephants. Like elephants, they were huge plant eaters. But mammoths had thick, shaggy fur.

The closest living relative of the woolly mammoth is the Asian elephant.

Icy Times

Early mammoths lived in Europe and Asia. Woolly mammoths came to North America during the last Ice Age. Huge sheets of ice called glaciers covered a lot of land.

Greenland

Ice Age glaciers

The Greenland Ice Sheet still covers most of the island of Greenland today.

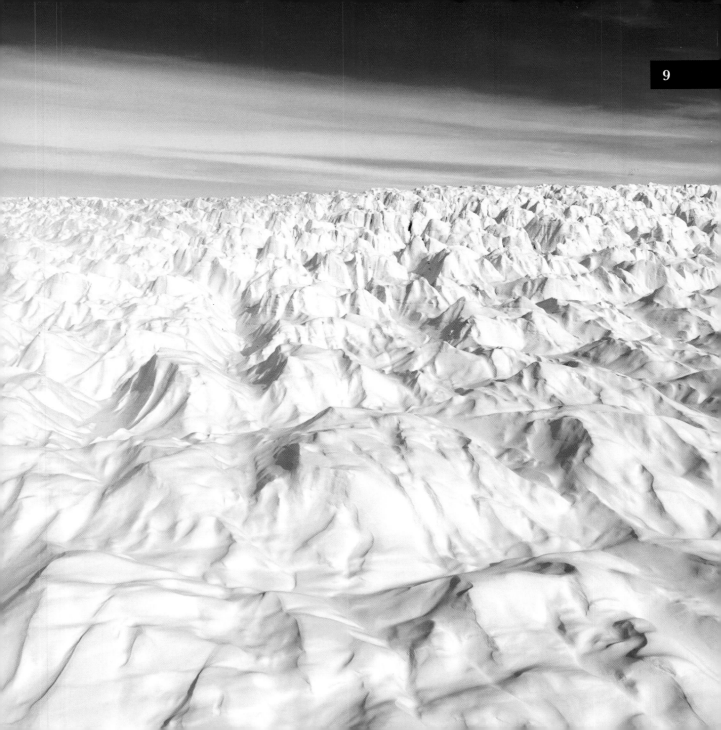

Mammoths ate short grasses, flowers, and other plants. But they were a food source for Ice Age *predators*. Dire wolves and saber-toothed cats hunted them.

Some types of mammoths, like imperial mammoths, weighed more than 10 tons (9.1 t)!

Frozen Plant Eaters

Woolly mammoths liked the cold. They lived in northern grasslands. They spent their days looking for food.

Plant eaters like mammoths are also known as herbivores.

Mammoth remains have been found in Russia, Europe, and farther north. Some of the bodies were trapped in ice. *Fossils* have been found as far south as South Dakota.

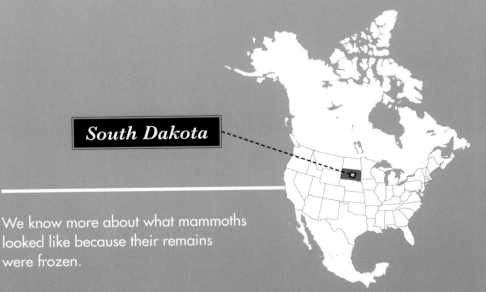

South Dakota

We know more about what mammoths looked like because their remains were frozen.

Useful Features

Mammoth *tusks* could be 15 feet (4.6 m) long! Tusks dug for food. They attracted mates. They could also be used to fight off some predators.

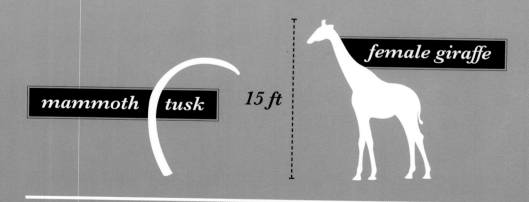

mammoth tusk   15 ft   female giraffe

The longest tusks were found on the biggest male woolly mammoths.

The fat on a mammoth's body helped keep it warm. Its long, thick fur was warm, too. An adult woolly mammoth weighed up to 6.6 tons (6 t).

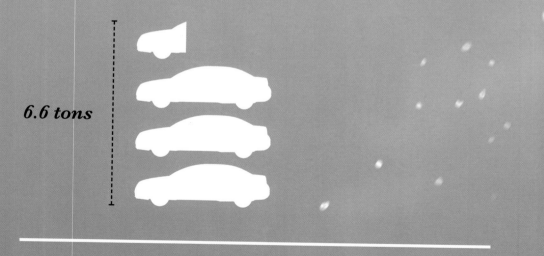

6.6 tons

Mammoths had four inches (10.2 cm) of fat under their skin and fur.

As the Ice Age ended, Earth got warmer. Mammoths could not find enough of the food they liked. Humans also hunted them for their fur and tusks. About 9,000 years ago, most mammoths died out.

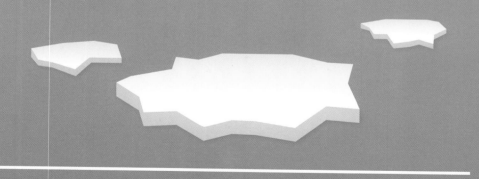

The very last mammoths lived on Wrangel Island until about 1700 B.C.

Mammoth Close-up

hump

fur

tusks

trunk

feet

Glossary

ancestors: relatives of modern animals

fossils: remains of animals or plants

predators: animals that hunt other animals
for food

tusks: two long teeth that stick out from an animal's
mouth

Read More

Miller, Debbie S. *A Woolly Mammoth Journey.* Fairbanks: University of Alaska Press, 2010.

Turner, Alan. *National Geographic Prehistoric Mammals.* Washington, D.C.: National Geographic, 2004.

Websites

Enchanted Learning: All about Mammoths
http://www.enchantedlearning.com/subjects /mammals/mammoth/
Read more about mammoths, take a quiz, and print out a coloring sheet.

National Geographic Kids: Woolly Mammoths
http://kids.nationalgeographic.com/animals /woolly-mammoth/#woolly-mammoth -standing.jpg
Find out more about woolly mammoths during the Ice Age.

Index